Universities and Innovation:
Meeting the Challenge

Ian Pearson is Member of Parliament for Dudley South and a
Visiting Fellow at the University of Warwick.

THE SOCIAL MARKET FOUNDATION

The Foundation's main activity is to commission and publish original papers by independent academic and other experts on key topics in the economic and social fields, with a view to stimulating public discussion on the performance of markets and the social framework within which they operate.

The Foundation is a registered charity and a company limited by guarantee. It is independent of any political party or group and is financed by the sales of publications and by voluntary donations from individuals, organisations and companies.

The views expressed in publications are those of the authors and do not represent a corporate opinion of the Foundation.

PATRONS
Viscount Chandos
Lord Flowers
Rt Hon Lord Owen CH
Lord Sainsbury of Turville

CHAIRMAN
Professor Lord Skidelsky FBA

MEMBERS OF THE ADVISORY COUNCIL
Professor Nick Bosanquet
Sir Samuel Brittan
Evan Davis
Michael Fallon MP
Liam Halligan
Professor John Kay
Lawrence Mone
Alex de Mont
Ian Pearson MP
Andrew Tyrie MP
John Willman
David Willetts MP

MEMBERS OF THE BOARD
Nick Alexander
Alex de Mont
Christopher Stone

DIRECTOR
Katharine Raymond

EDITORIAL CONSULTANT
Lord Kilmarnock

Universities and Innovation:
Meeting the Challenge

IAN PEARSON

The Social Market Foundation
March 2000

First published by The Social Market Foundation, 2000

The Social Market Foundation
11 Tufton Street
London SW1P 3QB

Copyright © The Social Market Foundation, 2000

The moral right of the authors has been asserted.

All rights reserved. Without limiting the rights under copyright reserved above, no part of this publication may be reproduced, stored or introduced into a retrieval system, or transmitted, in any form or by any means (electronic, mechanical, photocopying, recording, or otherwise), without the prior written permission of both the copyright owner and the publisher of this book.

ISBN 1 874097 47 X

Contents

Foreword by the Rt. Hon. Stephen Byers MP	i
Preface	iv
Introduction	1
The Knowledge Economy	6
Britain's Innovation Problem	11
Private Universities, State Benefits	24
The Government's Agenda	34
Further Areas For Action	39
Notes	54
Bibliography	61
SMF Papers	

Foreword
by the Secretary of State for Trade and Industry

The successful economies of the future will be those who are best at generating and exploiting knowledge. In the next 20 years there will be more innovation than at any time in the last 200.

Britain's future prosperity and well-being will depend on the ability of its businesses to compete in the knowledge driven economy. In a world swept by continuous change, they will have to continually adapt if they are to make profits, build shareholder value, and create wealth and jobs.

The new Labour government is working in partnership with business to create the right climate for innovation. A clear fiscal and monetary policy framework is locking in economic stability. We are stimulating greater competition, encouraging long-term investment, helping to equip people with the skills they need to succeed, and committed to regulating only when absolutely essential.

But in many ways we are only scraping the surface of what needs to be done in terms of our ambitions for Britain. We have to go much further in developing a programme of action to modernise the country. We need a programme that recognises that knowledge will be the global currency that really counts.

Everyone will be affected by the global changes ahead. If we are not going to be left behind we have to look at everything afresh. And we have to ensure our economic, social and political institutions are all aligned to the needs of the new economy.

In this controversial and thought-provoking paper, Ian Pearson MP looks at an important component of the knowledge economy - our universities - and what can be done to maximise the contribution they can make to our future economic performance.

Britain's science base is well-respected internationally. Our nation's university system has a reputation for academic excellence. We have some of the brightest minds and most creative people to be found anywhere in the world. But we have not done nearly well enough in exploiting the commercial potential of our ideas, particularly when compared with the United States.

Over the last two and a half years, government has already done a great deal to encourage universities and businesses to take a much closer interest in each other - and to improve our performance in bringing innovative ideas to the market.

- In partnership with the Wellcome Trust the science and engineering base is receiving a £1.4 billion boost.
- The University Challenge Fund is providing £50 million for early stage development of new ideas.
- Massachusetts Institute of Technology and Cambridge University are jointly establishing an Institute which will form a national network with the eight Centres of Excellence that we are establishing to equip scientists and engineers with entrepreneurship and business skills.
- The Reach Out Fund has been set up to help universities work more effectively with business.
- The DTI innovation budget has been increased by a fifth and successful initiatives - like the Teaching Company Scheme - expanded.
- More Faraday Partnerships are bringing together small businesses with scientists and engineers to develop profitable ideas.
- And the Foresight exercise is continuing to catalyse business and universities into looking at the future together.

But our ambition has to be to do more. We need a faster rate of innovation and learning. The challenge for business, universities and government is to come together and embrace change, not resist it. We need a new partnership focused on putting Britain on a path to sustainable growth and prosperity which takes full advantage of our academic knowledge base.

The paper Ian has produced offers a radical vision of a possible future for Britain's universities. It deserves scrutiny and discussion as part of the debate we need to be having on how our academic strengths can best help to contribute to our future economic success. It is a timely contribution as we look to produce a science and innovation policy to meet the challenges ahead.

The Rt. Hon. Stephen Byers MP
Secretary of State for Trade and Industry
December 1999

Preface

This report summarises the findings of a research project arising out of a long-standing interest of mine in why Britain's universities have been conspicuously less successful than their US counterparts in spawning the innovative new businesses of the future that will help shape and drive technological change in the new millennium.

Its aim is not just to identify where Britain has gone wrong, but to assess the significance of this poor track record for future economic performance, and to offer policy actions to bring about change.

In conducting the study, I am very grateful to Neil Skitt and to Michael Feinberg from the US who undertook much of the research. My thanks also go to Tom Goodwin, now at the UK Embassy in Japan, and Nick Matthews from the University of Warwick, for their comments and support. I would also like to thank Professor Kumar Bhattacharrya for his assistance, and Warwick for appointing me as a Visiting Fellow and enabling me to have the resources to complete the project.

Needless to say, most of the work in preparing this report has had to be done in spare time snatched after doing my normal day job. I hope nonetheless it stands up as a coherent analysis of why and where change is needed. Any errors, factual or otherwise, are obviously my responsibility.

Ian Pearson
Visiting Fellow, University of Warwick
December 1999

Introduction

Britain's universities have the potential to contribute significantly to the government's objectives of increasing growth and prosperity. By building stronger links with business, and through becoming more entrepreneurial and competitive, they have the ability to transform themselves into genuine universities for industry. This would produce macroeconomic benefits over the medium-term. It would also assist universities in the necessary process of upgrading and modernising themselves more generally, and does not require jettisoning long-standing reputations for academic excellence.

In bringing modern growth theory into the heart of policy-making, Britain's new Labour government has recognised the importance of knowledge as a source of economic growth. It has also stressed the need to tackle the productivity gap that exists with the US and France and Germany. Universities and innovation are evidently important in this context, but their roles and contributions are not always clearly understood. They are explored in this paper, which points out a number of areas where further action is needed.

While accepting that Britain needs to close the productivity gap with its competitors, it is important not to forget the product itself. Nissan in Sunderland is held to be the most productive car plant in the world, but it is discounting its cars because they cannot sell enough of them. Simply focusing on productivity and ignoring innovation - or lack of it - as a root cause of poor economic performance is making exactly the same mistake as the worst excesses of the Soviet planning regime where output was all that mattered. People have to want to buy and, for a wide range of market sectors, product differentiation through innovation is the key lever in creating effective demand.

Britain started the 1970s with some big national advantages: language, culture, and universities. Nevertheless, it failed to take advantage of the computer revolution. Its share of the world's IT market today is trivial and this can be only partly explained by the small size of the national IT market. Failures in other areas - where ideas originating in Britain have been successfully exploited commercially elsewhere - show there are deep-seated problems which need to be addressed if a genuinely innovative economy is to be re-created.

The study argues that Britain's innovation problem is largely the result of a poor performance in terms of patenting and exploiting new ideas and inventions; low levels of R&D expenditure both by business and by government; and misdirected government research priorities. These perpetuate Britain's reputation for being good at 'R' but bad at the 'D'.

Britain's innovative capacity is also constrained by its higher education sector not being sufficiently entrepreneurial. Traditionally, people in Britain have rightly been proud of its universities. Its elite institutions do well in most international comparisons, and its science base continues to produce research which is well-respected throughout the world. But Britain's elite universities are way off the pace compared with the US when it comes to developing links with business and acting entrepreneurially. MIT alone has generated nearly half as many spin-off businesses as all Britain's universities put together. Also, with the mass expansion of British higher education in the 1990s, and the abolition of the binary divide which saw the number of universities double, too little attention has been paid to the role of the non-elite universities. For most of them, they need to be differentiating themselves in the marketplace, not as research-led institutions but as industry-oriented trainers of the managers, professionals and technicians of the future.

There are several factors inhibiting our universities from contributing more fully to Britain's economic performance. The culture in Britain's elite universities - and many others - is still rather stuffy and not business-oriented. There is low competitive intensity in the sector. The problem of inadequate levels of research funding is compounded by the research 'jam' being spread far too thinly and the system being overlaid with bureaucracy. Research with industry, if not disparaged, is undervalued. There is a confusing array of government schemes promoting academic-business links, which is not well-understood by either party, and there is no expectation or incentive for academics to think commercially.

The new government's agenda on productivity and competitiveness has begun to address some of the constraints and inhibiting factors to innovation. It has recognised universities need to be better at commercially exploiting the knowledge base. Increases in funding for science and for the DTI's innovation budget are welcome steps in the right direction. So too is the R&D tax credit for companies to be implemented this year and the small funds which have been set up to encourage commercialisation of research and better academic-business interaction. Far more radical action is needed, however, if Britain is going to be able to maximise the potential of its higher education sector.

The report's final chapter identifies seven areas where further action is needed and suggests a range of initiatives which would contribute towards meeting the challenge of increasing the contribution Britain's universities can make to building an innovative economy:

- Promoting culture change and increasing competition between universities through: introducing detailed university league tables; reforming the funding system so it follows students more closely; invoicing students for the costs of their education; bringing in private companies to take over failing universities; stimulating the formulation of new private universities and joint ventures with the private sector; and promoting the importance of technological education.

- Stimulating greater business involvement by: having better marketed, simpler programmes for industry-academic collaboration; more business membership on university governing councils; improving the business content of science, engineering and IT courses; and transferring good practice in developing entrepreneurial links between universities and industry.
- Reforming government R&D funding by: shifting more funding to applied research and to tackling the development gap; concentrating it on fewer, high quality institutions; establishing ukinnovation.org as the first stop for all applied research and development, streamlining funding and programmes and giving them 'whoosh'; and stripping down and refocusing the Research Assessment Exercise.
- Encouraging and rewarding academic entrepreneurs through: changing academic contracts to build in time which it is expected will be spent on commercial work for their private benefit; financial incentive schemes to reward those bringing in private sector money to a department; reviewing and improving intellectual property policies to ensure they encourage spin-off businesses; and encouraging return tickets and easy-entries so there is fluidity between academia and the business world.
- Increasing exposure to business, design and technology in schools to give more pupils experience of these fields and to promote them as careers; extending work-related learning across the ability range; and utilising the New Deal for Schools to build expertise in teaching engineering.
- Improving government focus and co-ordination by giving a higher priority to innovation policy and to maximising the potential of universities; and establishing an inter-departmental Task Force and a powerful Cabinet sub-committee to facilitate stronger cross-departmental working.
- Supporting the growth of clusters through: ensuring universities clearly address their role in contributing to economic growth; encouraging more venture capital funds targeted at

commercialising university research; developing the infrastructure and networks to facilitate spin-off businesses, tasking the Small Business Service with supporting this, and getting universities to collaborate to increase their organisational capabilities so they have the critical mass to be able to identify and patent ideas and facilitate their development commercially; changing planning laws to allow clusters to develop; and expanding and creating more focused, high-quality science and research parks.

Meeting the challenge of maximising the contribution Britain's universities can make to growth and prosperity is an enormous task. It is hoped this study contributes to a greater understanding of why this is necessary and how Britain's government, its universities and the private sector can go about it together.

1. The Knowledge Economy

'A knowledge driven economy is one in which the generation and exploitation of knowledge has come to play the predominant part in the creation of wealth. It is not simply about pushing back the frontiers of knowledge; it is also about the more effective use and exploitation of all types of knowledge in all manner of economic activity.'

DTI, 1998 Competitiveness White Paper

Universities could play an important role in building the knowledge driven economy in Britain, acting as a driving force for improving national performance and prosperity. But too often the leading-edge knowledge they possess has remained locked away in ivory towers – or worse, transferred abroad – as others have been more entrepreneurial and innovative in exploiting its commercial potential.

Removing the barriers to innovation and stimulating entrepreneurship in Britain's higher education sector is not simple or straightforward and there are powerful vested interests involved. It will take time and commitment, but failing to tackle the problem is not an option if the nation's economic decline is to be reversed.

Productivity, growth and entrepreneurship
The growing importance of knowledge as a determinant of economic growth is now well-recognised.[1] The computer revolution, the explosion in information and communications technology, and scientific and technological advances are driving fundamental structural change worldwide. This has important implications for the competitiveness of nations – and repercussions for society – which

will increase in significance as the pace of knowledge-based competition intensifies.

The rise of the knowledge economy brings new challenges, necessitating businesses and nations to constantly re-examine the sources of their competitive advantage. Productivity is a fundamental yardstick. It is the key factor determining a nation's standard of living in the long run, since no economy can grow sustainably unless it increases productivity. But the role of knowledge in increasing productivity is all-too-often downplayed, as is the importance of entrepreneurship.

In Britain, poor labour productivity has been highlighted as the reason that the country lies at the bottom of the G7 league table in terms of output per capita.[2] The Government talks incessantly of a 40 per cent productivity gap with the US and 20 per cent with France and Germany. Tackling this gap is obviously a vital national task, the key question is what are the priorities.

The recent McKinsey Global Institute study[3] concluded that the root cause and most 'pervasive explanation' for low labour productivity lies in the effect of regulations governing product markets and land use on competitive behaviour, investment and pricing. It argued that low capital investment, poor skills and scale factors[4] were consequences of these restrictions. Many would dispute this. Although reforming regulations is important, its priority is questionable, as is the downgrading of other factors hampering productivity growth.

While low capital investment may indeed be 'largely the result of the lack of opportunities for profitable investment', there is a growing consensus that a more deeper explanation for this lies in the relatively high costs of capital, high 'hurdle' rates of return set for investment, and a failure in entrepreneurship and investing for the long-term. Similarly, their findings and justification for low skills levels being a secondary effect are unconvincing.[5]

Benchmarking British-based companies against the world's best in key market sectors, and focusing on spreading global best practice to improve productivity, as McKinsey advocate, should be commonplace. In the automotive sector, for instance, the inward investment of Nissan, Toyota, Honda and others – and with it the spread of Japanese working practices – has revolutionised productivity. But in tackling the productivity gap Britain has with its competitors, it is important not to forget the product itself. Nissan's plant in Sunderland is held to be the most productive car plant in the world. Yet Nissan is discounting its cars because it cannot sell enough of them. Simply focusing on productivity, and ignoring the product, is making exactly the same mistake as the worst excesses of the Soviet planning regime where output was all that mattered. People have to want to buy and, for a wide range of market sectors, product differentiation through innovation is a key factor in creating effective demand.

The government in Britain is right, therefore, in focusing its productivity strategy more broadly, establishing as priorities the need to address four of the nation's historic weaknesses: promoting innovation and enterprise; tackling the causes of under-investment; improving the skills base; and strengthening competition.[6] While there is not a seamless fit between its economic and industrial policy, there is certainly a substantial degree of co-ordination and a common understanding between the primarily Treasury-driven productivity agenda and the DTI focus on building the knowledge driven economy. This is based on modern growth theory and recognises the fundamental importance of knowledge and innovation.[7]

Competing through innovation
The 'essential character' of competition is innovation and change.[8] In the global economy, businesses and industries need to constantly improve and innovate – both in methods and technology – if they are to be successful. Innovation obviously comes in many forms. At the level of the firm, it could come from a new entrant to a market bringing new knowledge and skills. It need not involve complicated technology, and innovative firms are often not large, though they can

grow to become so. But, at the aggregate level, the evidence points to sustained research and development, and investment in human and financial capital, as important to the innovation process.

The key challenge for Britain is to become more innovative, since it is the entrepreneurial exploitation of new ideas, products and processes which helps drive productivity growth and is vital for economic prosperity. Experience indicates that there is no single path to building an innovative environment.[9] There are, however, examples and different models – Silicon Valley, Route 128, Tokyo – which are very familiar and offer some lessons.

In singling out universities, the study is focusing on only one of a number of forces that contribute to economic performance. The higher education sector is nonetheless a key ingredient in building a knowledge driven economy. It is a source of innovative ideas and it provides a flow of highly-trained people into the nation's workforce. With only possibly one or two exceptions, every successful 'innovative milieux' includes, or has included, universities as an essential component part.[10] Britain, therefore, needs a strongly entrepreneurial higher education sector if it is to be competitive. Universities, business and government all need to work effectively together to bring this about.

★ ★ ★ ★ ★ ★ ★ ★ ★ ★

Government has an important contribution to make in creating the innovative climate which is needed to ensure future prosperity. In Britain, the government's focus on knowledge and productivity is on the right lines but needs to be followed through consistently. Maximising the potential of the higher education sector must feature prominently on its agenda. As knowledge becomes ever more important to economic success, Britain has to compete through its universities as well as through its businesses.

The following sections of this report examine in more detail Britain's innovation problem, the state of the higher education sector, and the current government's policy on science and innovation. It concludes by identifying further areas for action.

2. Britain's Innovation Problem

Britain has the opportunity to become a substantially more innovative nation. From penicillin to the jet engine and liquid crystal display technology, there are countless examples of ideas and inventions generated in Britain being commercially exploited elsewhere. They are only the tip of the iceberg and indicate deep-seated problems which need to be addressed if a genuinely innovative economy is to be re-created.

Innovation takes many forms and is therefore difficult to measure in any comprehensive sense. This study highlights three key areas which indicate the size of Britain's innovation problem: its performance in terms of patenting new ideas and inventions; levels of R&D expenditure both by business and by government; and government research priorities.

Falling behind on patents

Britain is not particularly effective in turning ideas generated through research and other sources into products and processes which it then exploits commercially.[1] It is losing out in the innovation race and this is hampering economic performance.[2] Starting with the patenting of new ideas, international comparisons show that Britain's share of US and EU patents lags substantially behind our major competitors (Chart 2.1).

Different national regulations and measurement systems mean that caution must be exercised in making international comparisons. Britain's low share of US and EU patents is just one indicator of its innovation problem – and, clearly, attempts at solutions must involve more than just registering more ideas as patents.

Chart 2.1: Share of US and EU Patents in 1995

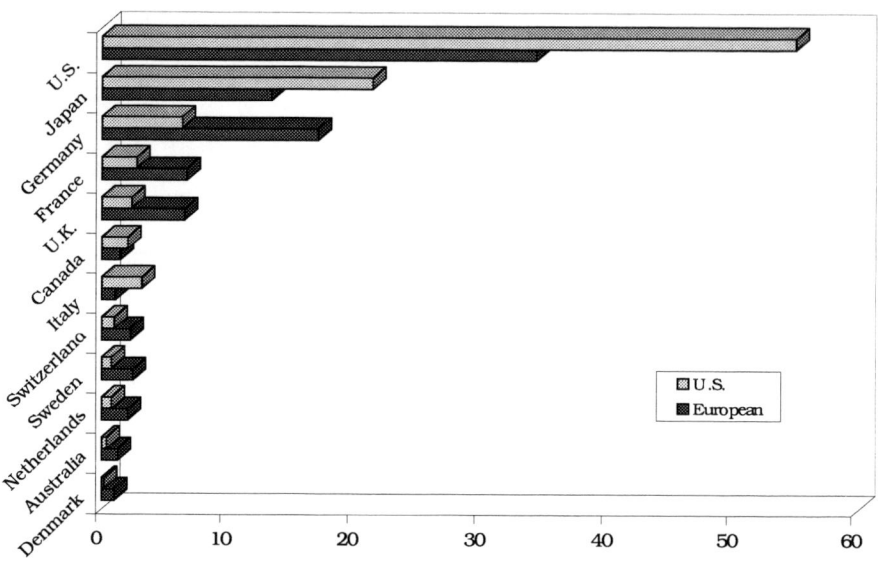

SOURCE: Science, 3 July 1998

Evidence suggests, however, that data on international patenting per capita is a good indicator of future prosperity and explains a high proportion of the variance in innovative output across countries.[3] Britain performs even less well according to this criterion, ranking way behind Japan and the US with Germany also well ahead (Chart 2.2).

Chart 2.2: International Per Capita Patenting Performance in 1996

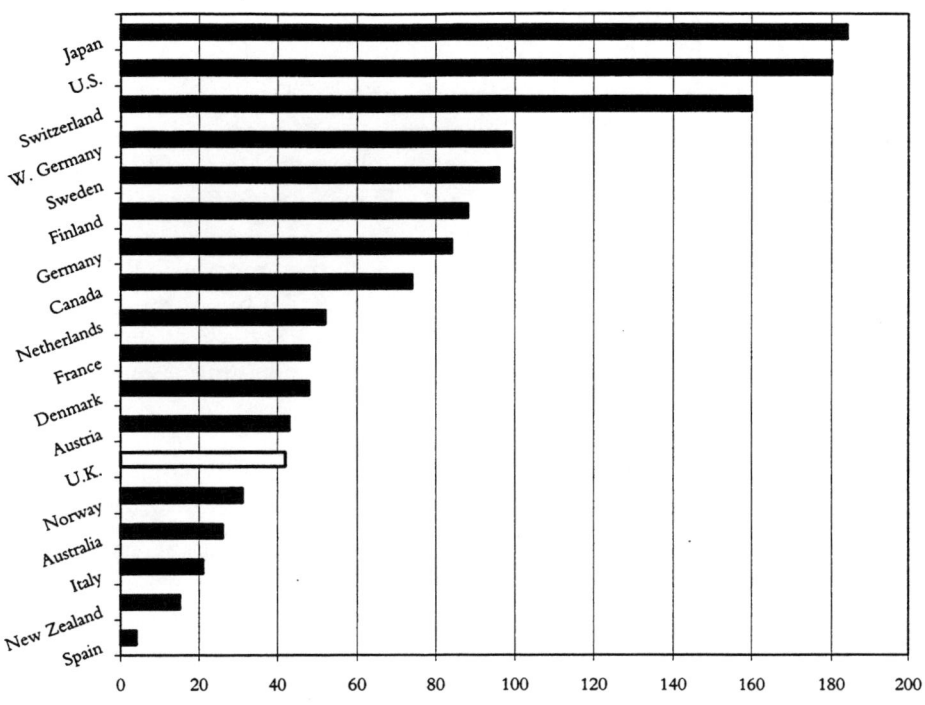

SOURCE: Porter (1998)

It is important to realise that this poor performance is not a 'one-off' or a recent phenomenon. Britain's patent record has been roughly flat at this low level for over twenty years. In contrast, US and Japanese performance increased steadily during the 1980s and 1990s.[4]

While too much emphasis should not be placed on the fact that Britain has fallen and is falling behind on patents, it is nevertheless a significant variable, and other available indicators all point in the same direction. Together they demonstrate that Britain's innovation problem is both deep-rooted and long-term.

Low levels of R&D

Converting ideas generated through research and development into patents is clearly important. Notwithstanding this, overall levels of R&D expenditure are also a prime determinant of innovative capacity. As has been well-documented elsewhere, however, Britain lags substantially behind the US, Japan, France and Germany in terms of total R&D expenditure.[5]

Taking both the public and private sectors together, Britain's gross expenditure on R&D in 1997 totalled £14.7 billion or 1.8 per cent of GDP. But, as a proportion of GDP, the US and Japan invest about 50 per cent more in R&D than Britain, and France and Germany both around 20 per cent more. Moreover, with the exception of Germany, this R&D gap has remained broadly stable or increased over the last ten years (Chart 2.3).

The problem in Britain lies both with low business investment and low government R&D expenditure. While different national R&D structures mean that care must be taken in making international comparisons it is, nevertheless, clear that taking a fifteen year span business R&D spending has, on average, been 75 to 100 per cent higher in Japan, 40 to 70 per cent higher in Germany and at least 30 to 50 per cent higher in the US, even though US figures exclude most capital expenditure.

Government R&D spending in Britain was on a par with German levels from 1983-87 but has declined substantially since, with German government R&D expenditure now 37 per cent higher. Government R&D spending in France has throughout been significantly higher than in Britain (Chart 2.4).

Chart 2.3: Trends in gross R&D expenditure in G7 countries

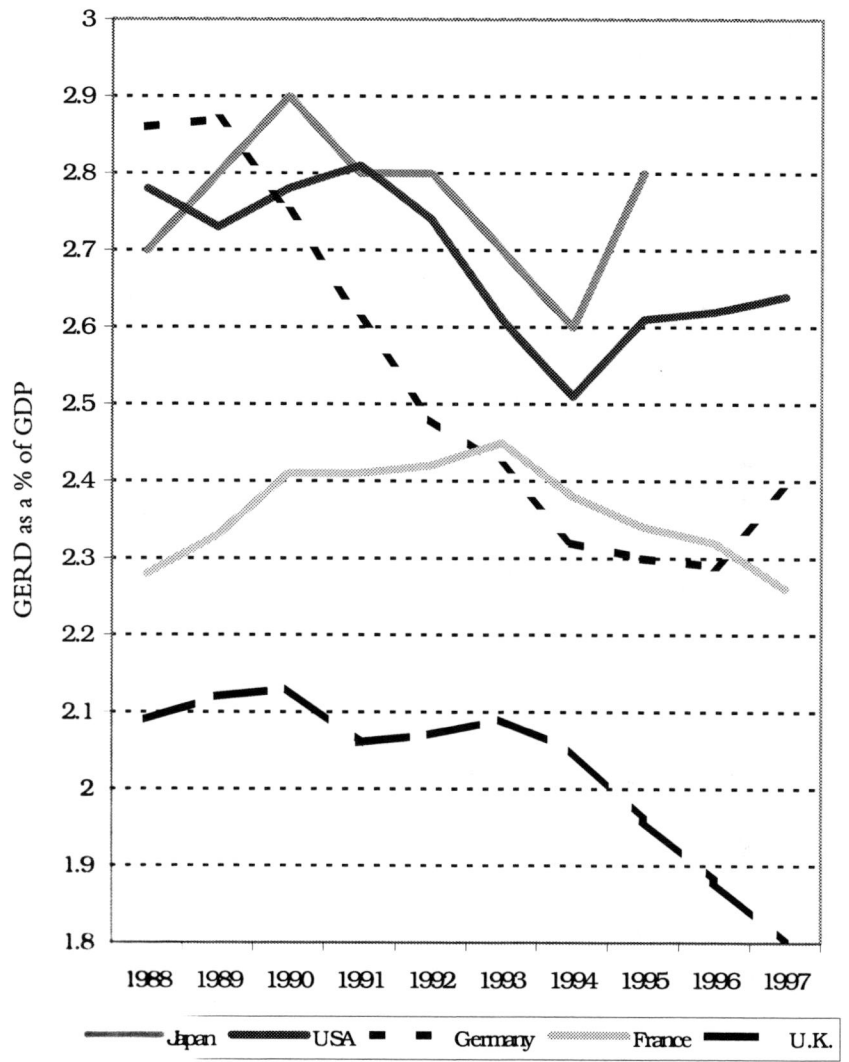

SOURCE: SET Statistics, 1999, Table 7.1

Chart 2.4: Gross R&D expenditure by source as a percentage of GDP in selected countries

Average 1983 to 1987	UK	Germany	France	Japan	USA
Government	0.93	0.98	1.17	0.5	1.35
Business Enterprise	1.01	1.65	0.92	1.83	1.39
Other	0.25	0.04	0.12	0.18	0.05
Total	**2.19**	**2.67**	**2.21**	**2.51**	**2.79**

Average 1988 to 1992	UK	Germany	France	Japan	USA
Government	0.72	0.94	1.13	0.47	1.17
Business Enterprise	1.06	1.7	1.04	2.13	1.51
Other	0.31	0.07	0.2	0.17	0.09
Total	**2.09**	**2.71**	**2.37**	**2.77**	**2.77**

Average 1993 to 1997	UK	Germany	France	Japan	USA
Government	0.63	0.86	0.8	0.32	0.91
Business Enterprise	0.96	1.44	0.91	1.18	1.58
Other	0.36	0.05	0.64	0.11	0.1
Total	**1.96**	**2.34**	**2.35**	**1.62**	**2.6**

SOURCE: SET Statistics, 1999, Table 7.3

Low business investment by British companies, compared with those in other countries, is also shown through the R&D Scoreboard.[6] Britain has only 19 companies in the world top 300 ranked by R&D spending and together their expenditure as a percentage of sales is 50 per cent below the G7 average (Chart 2.5).

Chart 2.5: R&D Scoreboard: international comparisons with selected countries

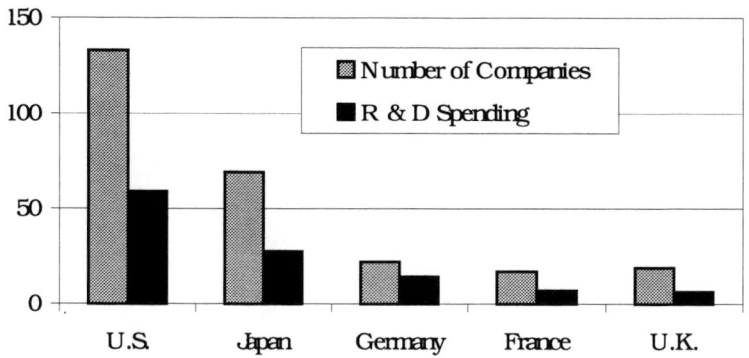

SOURCE: R&D Scoreboard 1998

R&D expenditure as a percentage of sales

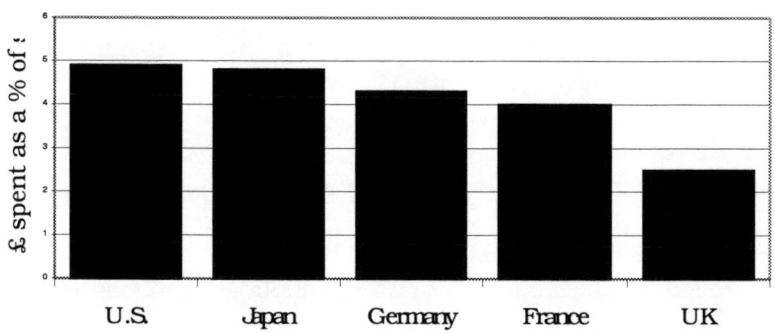

SOURCE: R&D Scoreboard 1998

Government R&D investment in Britain is not only low in international comparison. Total government-funded civil R&D expenditure (i.e. excluding defence) is less in real terms than it was a decade ago. It declined by over 10 per cent from 1986 to 1991 and is not projected to get back to 1986 levels until 2000-01 (Chart 2.6).

Chart 2.6: Net Government civil R&D expenditure in real terms 1986 to 2002

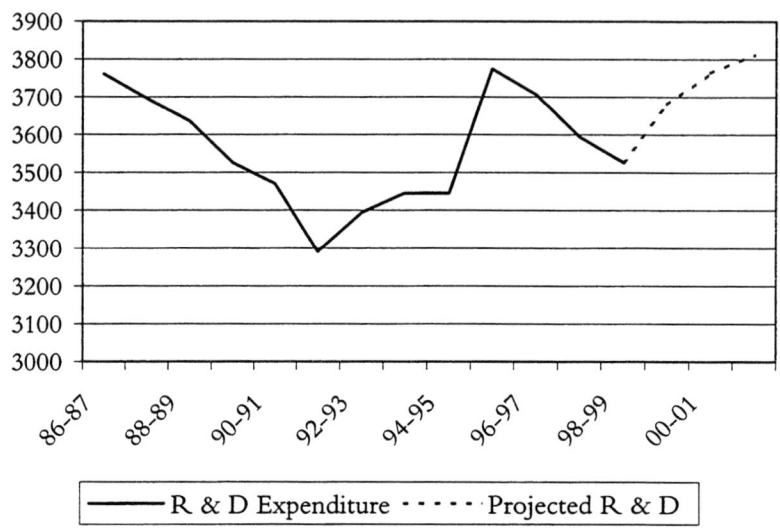

SOURCE: SET Statistics, 1999, Table 3.2

Mis-directed research priorities

Britain's comparatively low government R&D spending is further diluted by focusing on areas not likely to produce tangible economic benefits. Clearly, governments should not fund research that should be funded by industry itself. Any responsible government also has to look to the long-term and be prepared to fund research to advance knowledge for its own sake. Technological progress often has its foundations in research conducted initially without any thought for its commercial potential. The issue for Britain is whether it has got the balance right. Evidence suggests that it could do much better at ensuring that government-funded research is included in the supply chain for the knowledge driven economy, so that its output can be harnessed for wealth creation.

Government-funded R&D expenditure in 1997-98 was just under £6.3 billion. Defence accounts for slightly over one third of this expenditure, as does spending on the science and engineering base through the Research Councils and Higher Education Institutions. Expenditure by civil departments accounts for nearly a further fifth, with the remainder being accounted for by Britain's contribution towards EU R&D spending (Chart 2.7).

Chart 2.7: Government funded R&D expenditure 1997-98

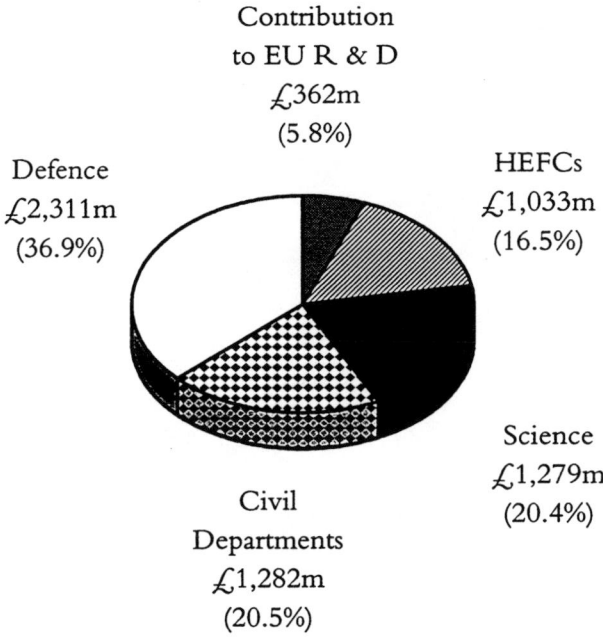

SOURCE: SET Statistics, 1999, Table 3.1

However, less than a third of the total government-funded research council and civil R&D expenditure is classified as spending on specific applied research, which has specified products or processes as its aims; or on experimental development, drawing on existing knowledge to produce new materials, products or processes, systems or services (Chart 2.8).

Chart 2.8: Net Government Research Council and Civil R&D expenditure by research activity in 1997-98

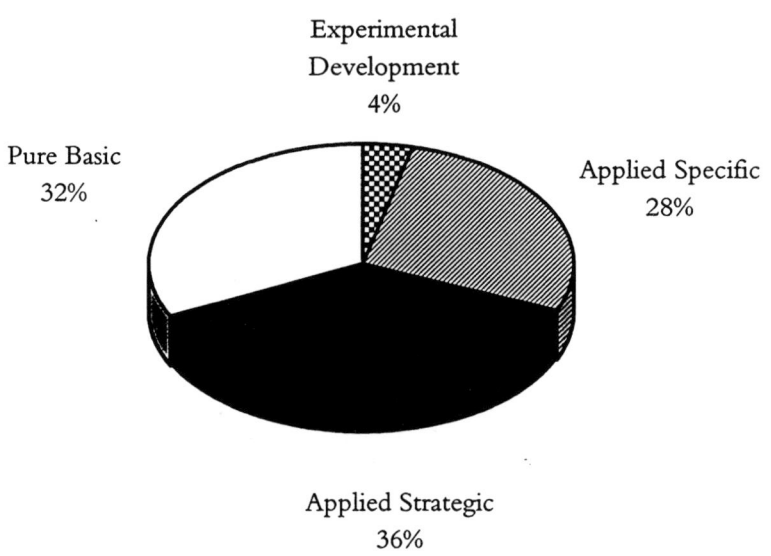

SOURCE: SET Statistics, 1999, Table 3.4

And the trend in Research Council R&D spending over the last decade has seen basic 'blue skies' research increase its share of total expenditure from 50 to 60 per cent. This has primarily been at the expense of strategic applied research,[7] although this still accounts for around one third of the total. What is most evident, however, is that very little Research Council funded expenditure is directed towards anything that is most likely to be near market (Chart 2.9).

Chart 2.9: Trends in net Research Council R&D expenditure by research activity

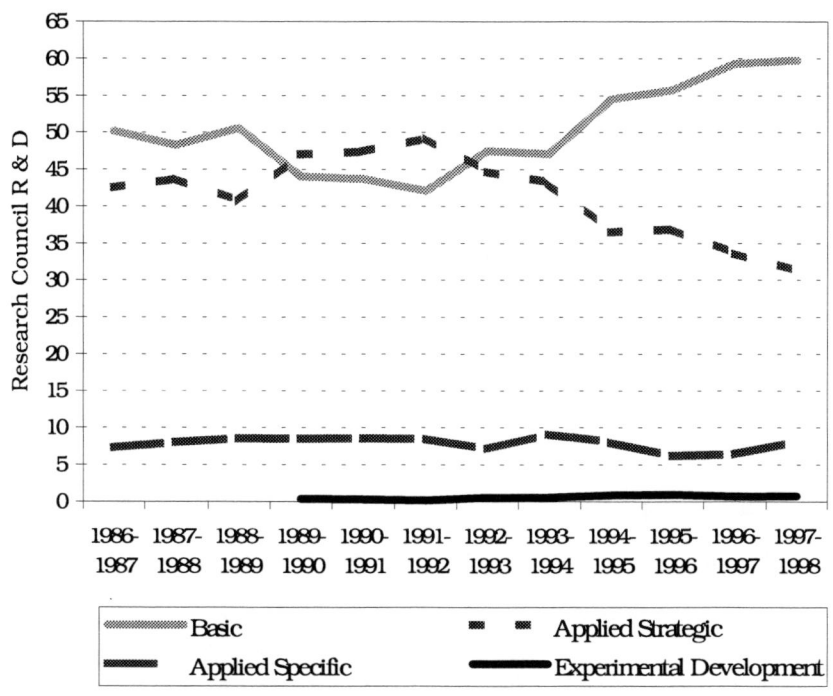

SOURCE: SET Statistics, 1999, Table 3.4

Trends in the composition of R&D funded by the civil departments show strategic applied research doubling - increasing from 22 per cent of the total in 1986-87 to 46 per cent in 1996-97. This has been at the expense of nearer market experimental development which has declined from just over a quarter of the total in 1986-87 to just 7 per cent in 1997-98.[8]

Overall, very little of Britain's government-funded R&D is specifically targeted towards industry. Of the nearly £6.3 billion total of government-funded R&D expenditure in 1997-98 only a pitifully low 1.7 per cent is classed as having the objective of industrial development. Amazingly, this has declined from 10.5 per cent just over a decade ago (Chart 2.10).

The current orientation towards basic and applied strategic research may be appropriate to the needs of Britain's pharmaceutical industries and they are well plugged into the current system. For industries based in engineering and the physical sciences, however, a different research funding balance is required.

The reality is that Britain has a world-class science base which is 'blue skies' rather than industry oriented. Government has a role in encouraging basic science, but any government needs to have other objectives in terms of developing and exploiting new technologies commercially as well. In Britain, government R&D funding is bolstering a flagging academic reputation at the expense of more commercial objectives. This is contributing to the development gap Britain has with its competitors.

★ ★ ★ ★ ★ ★ ★ ★ ★ ★ ★

Britain is poor at turning inventions into innovations and exploiting them commercially. The main reasons for Britain's innovation problem are low levels of business and government R&D expenditure and a poor performance of converting research ideas into patented products and processes. Government research expenditure is also not well-targeted on areas most likely to produce economic benefits. Improving Britain's performance in these areas would help the economy to be substantially more innovative.

Chart 2.10: Net Government R&D expenditure by socio-economic objectives

Government Expenditure (%)	86-87	87-88	88-89	89-90	90-91	91-92	92-93	93-94	94-95	95-96	96-97	97-98
Agriculture, Forestry and Fishing	4.7	4.5	4.7	4.1	4	4.3	5.1	5.3	5.1	5	4.5	4.6
Industrial Development	10.5	9.4	8.9	9.5	9.7	7.9	7.8	8.5	3.5	2.9	2.5	1.7
Energy	4.4	3.9	3.9	3.3	2.9	2.6	2.4	1.8	1.1	0.9	0.7	0.7
Infrastructure	1.5	1.5	1.5	1.5	1.5	1.3	1.7	1.8	1.9	1.7	1.7	1.7
Environmental Protection	1.1	1.3	1.3	1.1	1.4	1.4	1.4	2	2.3	2.3	2.2	2.3
Health	4.5	4.6	4.9	5.5	5.9	5.9	6.7	7.1	7.6	13.5	14.5	14.4
Social Development and Services	1.5	1.6	2.1	2.1	2.2	2.3	2.8	2.8	2.7	2.4	2.1	1.9
Earth and Atmosphere	1.9	1.9	2.2	2.6	2.9	2.9	2.4	1.8	2.1	1.9	1.7	1.4
Advancement of Knowledge	21.5	22.8	23.3	22.1	22.7	24	25.6	22.9	31.4	29.6	29.7	28.9
Civil Space	2.9	3	3.3	3.1	3.1	2.7	2.9	3.5	3.1	2.7	2.8	2.8
Defence	45.1	45.2	43.5	44.7	43.5	43.9	40.8	42	38.9	36.5	37.2	39.2
Not Elsewhere Classified	0.3	0.3	0.3	0.3	0.2	0.7	0.5	0.6	0.4	0.4	0.4	0.4
TOTAL	100	100	100	100	100	100	100	100	100	100	100	100

SOURCE: SET Statistics, 1999, Table 3.8

3. Private Universities, State Benefits

People in Britain have traditionally been proud of its universities. The country's elite institutions do well in most international comparisons and its science base continues to produce research which is well-respected throughout the world. But Britain's top universities are way off the pace compared with the United States when it comes to developing links with businesses and acting entrepreneurially. The rest are little better and need to more clearly differentiate their mission and distinctive competencies.

This study examines a number of barriers to creating more academic entrepreneurs and more entrepreneurial universities. Evidence is drawn from Britain and the US and, by their very nature, tend to be illustrative rather than definitively based on statistics. Nevertheless, it strongly suggests that academic culture, the level of competition between universities, course content and structure, the status of science and engineering, incentives to work in partnership with industry or start businesses, patent policies, and related infrastructure and networks to support clusters, are all areas which need to be addressed, along with the role of government itself.

Slow to modernise
Higher education in Britain has changed out of all recognition since the early 1960s. It might seem counter-intuitive, therefore, to argue that the sector has been slow to modernise. In many important areas, however, it has not moved as far or as fast as in other advanced nations.

Following the post-Robbins growth of the late Sixties,[1] the 1988-93 period saw a further massive increase in student numbers. This coincided with the abolition of the 'binary divide' in 1992 when the former polytechnics became incorporated as universities. The sector is now extremely diverse, making generalisations difficult. However, it is clear that pressures in the system are making all institutions try to be more like each other, which is bad news for future economic performance.

In 1996/97 there were over 1.6 million registered students in Britain, with over 1.1 million of these studying full-time. Much of the increase since the 1960s has been women. They now make up half the student population compared with only a quarter 30 years ago. Participation has widened but is still class-related. Participation by young people from semi-skilled and unskilled families is low. Less than 10 per cent of those from socio-economic groups IV and V go into higher education in contrast to around 80 per cent of those from group I. At the same time, however, postgraduate study has more than doubled, increasing from 6 per cent to 14 per cent of the total student population.[2]

The Dearing committee of inquiry noted that Britain's higher education institutions can take 'justifiable pride' in what it has achieved over the last 30 years.[3] This may be true but the sector is still at a crossroads if not in crisis. The inquiry's recommendations on the purposes, shape, structure, size and funding of higher education over the next 20 years have been partially implemented by government. Its remit was relatively limited, however, and its analysis is certainly not the last word on the subject.

Too many of Britain's universities have tried to follow the traditional model of being both teaching and research institutions. What is more they have, by and large, been allowed to do this by government. Government research funding has been spread fairly widely with two out of five British universities receiving research funding at some level. In contrast, only one in twenty universities in the US get government research backing. The peer review process is largely responsible for this. In Britain it can be like the world's worst remuneration committee, with friends rewarding friends, rather than tough decisions being taken to concentrate resources. The whole funding system is also massively bureaucratic.

Evidence suggests that the more focused approach to research funding in the US produces better results. Coupling this with the need to rebalance existing government R&D funding in Britain to concentrate more on applied research and development, as indicated earlier, clearly demonstrates that a fundamental shift in policy direction is required. More universities need to be encouraged, or made, to concentrate exclusively on their teaching role. They should take pride in training the technicians, managers and professionals of tomorrow, and not engage in futile attempts to 'ape' the elite institutions who mainly have long-standing research reputations.

The current university funding system in Britain does not help these changes to take place. Higher education is heavily regulated and planned. Growth in student numbers is only available through various bids, with the numbers concerned often in areas of the market where there is no evidence at all that the demand for additional places actually exists. The funding methodology also reinforces the status quo. As one university Vice Chancellor puts it, 'if this university, or any other, decided that it could improve the efficiency with which it taught students and as a result took more students at a lower unit cost, the funding methodology means that we would be fined for the improvement in the value for money that we were giving to the public. We would be required to reduce our student intakes until we had received the same level of inefficiency as every other university in the country.'

Some still deny it but Britain has conspicuously lagged behind other nations when it comes to technical and business education. Britain's first colleges of advanced technology opened in 1963, some 120 years after Germany's. Its first two business schools opened in 1965 and 1966, nearly 200 years after Harvard.[4] Cambridge did not establish a business school until 1990 and Oxford only in 1996. Moreover, too often the focus has been on 'abstract education' which has not provided good training for industrial research and 'seldom proved of industrial value'.[5] The problem has been that Britain's education culture has stressed humanities and science over more practical pursuits and, as a result, its workforce is behind other advanced nations in technical education and skills, with very few top managers having a technical background.[6]

Of course, the contribution of other disciplines to the wealth creation should not be ignored. The humanities, literacy and languages are all obviously important. While the study has focused on science, engineering and the IT base, it must be recognised that technological innovation and advance cannot flourish when its practitioners can neither write nor think logically. Communication skills require a sophisticated use of language. Marketing can only benefit from a knowledge of other cultures and other languages. But, overall, while Britain's universities have done a lot to promote civilisation, the disappointing fact is that they have done a lot less to promote business.

The contrast with universities in the United States is glaring. From top to bottom there is a radically more competitive culture and business orientation. The 'Ivy League' universities are far more open to business than Oxbridge or the 'red brick' universities, while the state universities tend to be much more focused and entrepreneurial than their British counterparts. In some ways this is because they are further down the track of engaging the private sector. Since the 1970s most places of higher education in the US have been campaigning for the nation's best and brightest students in an increasingly systematic and businesslike fashion. Private sector funding, from business and Alumni, has been instrumental in enabling universities to compete through offering upgraded, state-of-the-art facilities.[7] Businesses, meanwhile, have recognised for a long time that universities can be a bastion of new ideas and potentially profitable new products, as well as bright recruits.

Moreover, going into business after university – and frequently while still at it – is very much the 'norm' in the US. Business is part of the academic curriculum in colleges and universities. In Britain the implicit message is that business is for academic failures. Business does not really feature as part of the school curriculum, and there is a low penetration of quality business linkages at secondary level, with only around 60,000 of 3 million 12-18 year olds participating in the three significant schemes available.[8]

Examination of course content and structures at selected universities also shows that business features significantly more prominently in engineering courses in US universities compared with British ones. The links with business through extramural programmes and seminars are also far more extensive in the US. Stanford runs courses in Selected Entrepreneurial Issues and High-Tech Entrepreneurship. Many of the very brightest students choose Stanford over Harvard, Yale and the others because they recognise the future career opportunities that will arise from studying engineering there.[9]

In Britain, the relatively low status accorded to engineering and poor pay prospects does not help. It is a well-recognised problem. Surveys regularly show that the City and the professions are more attractive occupations for top graduates than business and this feeds through to decisions taken by students applying to universities. This anti-business, anti-engineering bias is reinforced by historical factors. Despite numerous campaigns and initiatives, the image of engineering as something 'dirty' still persists in the minds of prospective students. It may be wrong but it is extremely difficult to shake off.[10]

Poor links with industry
While there are many examples of links between universities and industry in Britain, they are not on anything like the same scale that is found in a typical American science, engineering or business school. It is not just a problem of undergraduate courses having an insufficient business orientation. It runs through to corporate sponsorship of faculty posts and facilities, where the US is way ahead,

and it includes joint research projects and the potential to link with existing businesses and 'spin out' new innovative companies.

Britain's traditional universities have had 'a notoriously weak capacity to steer themselves' which has become more debilitating as the pace of change in the sector has accelerated.[11] The decision-making structures of some of the top universities are a powerful force for inertia. Elsewhere the response of universities to financial pressures has been patchy with some of them reacting in a deeply unambitious manner. Management groups and academic departments in Britain's universities have little or no incentive, however, to embrace change and bring in private sector sponsorship and projects. They have safe, albeit relatively poorly paid jobs, and a good pension scheme. In contrast, administrators and faculty in most US universities have direct financial incentives to bring in industry funding and support. Deans and faculty can reap the rewards of bringing in business funding through performance bonuses.

At the individual research level, there is also no real incentive to develop industry links. Working with industry is at the bottom of the academic food chain in Britain. The current system sends out clear signals that if you want to get on the best thing to do is to publish work in refereed academic journals, teaching comes next, with collaborative research with industry at the bottom of the pile. Again the contrast with the US is stark. Publish or perish is well-understood there too, after all they invented it, but working with business – or setting up one or more of your own – is expected and positively encouraged.

Judging by a recent memorandum from Cambridge University the situation is not getting any better. It reported 'growing pressures on staff in the University make it increasingly difficult for them to find time to commercialise science and technology. In a time of rigorous research assessment, patents and other forms of commercialisation are not recognised as research outputs. The formality of research and teaching demands is increasing and the scope for spontaneity may be less. 'Death by accountability' is a real danger.'[12]

In Britain there is a 'bewildering array'[13] of government programmes to fund collaborative research between industry. Some of these appear on the face of it to be fairly successful. Both the Teaching Company Scheme and the LINK programme have been favourably evaluated.[14] They are however relatively small-scale initiatives, not particularly well promoted, and for many companies it is just too much trouble to get involved. The widespread view is that such a large number of schemes is confusing.[15] They generate huge levels of bureaucracy and have led to calls for a more streamlined system.

Poor links with industry is one of the reasons for Britain's poor patenting performance, which, as noted earlier, contributes to its innovation problem. A recent survey in the US found that half of the industry patents filed cited university research as the initial source of inspiration. The figure for Britain is not available but, almost certainly, would be much lower. The study found recent improvements taking place in both the numbers of universities with policies on intellectual property and the quality of patent policies. Some catching up is still required but a number of British universities have adopted patent sharing agreements similar to those at Stanford and other leading US universities where income is shared between the individual, the host department and the university. Similarly, a number of universities have companies or organisations whose purpose is to support the commercialisation of research.[16] However, these are way behind where the leading universities in the US are in terms of systematically exploiting research and turning inventions into profit. Most employ only a few people and the impression is that they do not have the critical mass of somewhere like Stanford. As they stand, they do not appear likely to help produce the radical gear-shift that is needed to improve Britain's innovation performance.

The establishment of science or research parks near to universities is another way in which universities develop and extend industry links. They can play an important part in building industry clusters.

Britain has again followed the lead of the US and there have been some striking successes. These parks work best in economic development terms where they stick to their original remit, and there are clear, tangible links between the businesses on those sites and university departments and research staff. Evidence suggests, however, that many in the UK have gradually drifted away from this goal. Under commercial pressure to keep up occupancy rates, science parks have let space to companies with no links to the university. This trend is continuing and is making them more like any other high-quality business park. While this is no bad thing in itself, it means Britain is missing out on the potential benefits that academic-industry links can bring through establishing these mechanisms.

Low pay and competition
University salaries in Britain are low compared to other occupations and simply not competitive internationally. There has been virtually no increase in the real earnings of university lecturers over the last 20 years, while average earnings have increased by over 36 per cent during this period.[17] This is already having an effect on the quality of the academic labour force. Some of the very best have voted with their feet. For years there has been a significant 'brain-drain' to the US in 'hot' topics. Anybody really good has to accept that they will lose out financially if they decide to become an academic. Not surprisingly, fewer and fewer are choosing to do so. Trying to entice top academics from the US is virtually impossible. One leading British academic has said 'Americans laugh at us; they just laugh at us' as they are on 'two and a half times the salary' of their British counterparts.[18]

Britain's elite universities are under international threat. It is not just that they are losing or not attracting the brightest and best academic minds, their very status as pre-eminent institutions is in jeopardy. To compete better internationally, they need to first become better at competing nationally. In British academic circles the widely held view is that there is vigorous competition for students, for faculty and for research funding and sponsorship. It is wrong.

The reality is that competition in Britain's university sector is at a low level. In the United States universities go out and sell themselves to high school graduates. Competition for private sector cash and for staff is fierce and sometimes nasty.[19]

Other countries are already recognising the benefits of allowing the private sector to collaborate and compete with existing universities. At least nine private universities are to be launched in Germany. This is already provoking competition which will move the sector forward. Leading academics are backing some of the initiatives, many of which are joint ventures. The International University of Bremen brings together Bremen University, the state government and the private Rice University of Houston, Texas. The computer software firm, SAP, is involved in the International University in Bruchsal, Baden Württemberg. In Australia, Melbourne University has set up a private company as an offshoot whose principal objective is profit.[20]

Apart from Buckingham University, founded in the 1970s, Britain has no private universities. With the changes that have taken place nationally and internationally over the past decade, it is missing out on opportunities for innovation as a result. Recently, it was announced that Nord Anglia, a private company, is to offer two-year business degree courses which will be validated by Oxford Brookes University. Such moves can only help increase choice and lead to improved products and standards. However, there are legal barriers in the way of greater private sector involvement, and it is high time these were reviewed.

For years British universities have been squeezed financially by government which has encouraged the ratcheting up of student numbers but has not wanted to pay for it. Newly introduced tuition fees will bring in extra resources, but a flat rate fee system, irrespective of where you go to university, is hardly sustainable in the long-term and will have to change. Bringing in private sector resources to make up the difference and increasing competition to make the sector more efficient have got to be the way forward.

★ ★ ★ ★ ★ ★ ★ ★ ★

Britain's universities have been slow to modernise and bring in the private sector. They are falling behind internationally and government has been little or no help. Removing the barriers to creating more entrepreneurial universities, and to encouraging more academic entrepreneurs, would enable the potential the higher education sector has to create and support growth and prosperity in the economy to be maximised.

4. The Government's Agenda

'The UK needs to enhance a first-rate science base, putting proper systems in place for exploiting the commercial value of research, and getting scientists and business to take a much closer interest in each other'

HM Treasury (1998)

For more than a decade, successive governments in Britain have preached the importance of enterprise and competitiveness. The need to exploit the country's science base more fully – and to be more innovative – has routinely featured in politicians' rhetorical flourishes. But until recently this talk has not been translated into action and the role of universities in the wealth generation process has been largely ignored.

The new Labour government's agenda is a major step forward. A coherent policy framework has been established which is underpinned by a clear understanding of the importance of knowledge to growth and prosperity. Within this context the study highlights the main new initiatives taken or planned by government. It concludes however that Britain is still lagging behind its major competitors and that more radical action is needed.

Competitiveness

The new British government's economic strategy rightly has as its centrepiece a commitment to macroeconomic stability and to using 'supply side' measures to promote enterprise and investment. Its focus on knowledge, skills and creativity as a means of closing the productivity gap Britain has with its competitors is firmly grounded in modern growth theory which provides the framework for its actions.

A raft of measures have been announced since the May 1997 general election relating to this competitiveness agenda. These include reducing rates of corporation tax, changes to the capital gains tax regime and to competition policy, a new £20 million venture capital challenge to finance early high technology businesses, and from this year a new R&D tax credit for companies and a new employee share ownership scheme.[1]

Other initiatives underway, such as the formation of the Small Business Service, the University for Industry, individual learning accounts, and the planned post-16 changes to education and training, are also part of the competitiveness agenda and will impinge on universities and innovation. The Regional Development Agencies are, to some extent, starting to do this already. Many of them are focusing on supporting the development of clusters, in which universities should play a key role. Government itself has appointed a Minister responsible for the 'nationally important' biotechnology cluster, most of which is located around Cambridge.[2]

Innovation and science
The biggest government announcement relating specifically to universities has been the boosting of the science budget by £1.4 billion in partnership with the Wellcome Trust. This is a significant new commitment, though most of this will go on new equipment and buildings - bringing up to date an infrastructure that was looking increasingly 'creaky'. It does nothing in itself to deal with Britain's poor track record of commercialising research and spinning out new businesses. All it does is get somewhere nearer levelling the playing field with countries like France and Germany on the 'hardware' side.

Further initiatives are beginning to address some of the issues identified earlier in the study. For instance, the University Challenge fund is providing £50 million early stage funding to help exploit the commercial potential of research, and greater awareness of business amongst academics is being encouraged through a £25 million Science Enterprise Challenge fund. There is a £20 million 'reach

35

out' fund to encourage more interaction with business in England, and similar arrangements for Scotland and Wales. The Teaching Company Scheme is being doubled and previous initiatives like Faraday Partnerships and the Foresight programme are being built on and extended.[3]

SCIENCE-BUSINESS INITIATIVES SINCE MAY 1997

- an extra £1.4 billion over three years, in partnership with the Wellcome Trust, to spend on modernising the science and engineering base
- 20 per cent increase in DTI's innovation budget over three years
- £50 million University Challenge Fund for early stage development of ideas with commercial potential
- £20 million per year reach out fund to help English universities work more effectively with business (£34 million in Scotland)
- up to eight new enterprise centres at leading universities, to equip scientists and engineers with entrepreneurship and business skills, through the £25 million Science Enterprise Challenge programme
- Teaching Company Scheme doubled, enabling around 200 extra projects per year to be backed
- a national network of Faraday Partnerships which each bring together up to 40 innovating small businesses with scientists and engineers to share ideas and commercialise research
- new round of the Foresight programme
- £10 million for a second round of Foresight Link awards to promote partnerships between universities and business

---

The new initiatives are along the right lines and a move towards creating an innovation policy and not just a science and technology policy.[4] However, apart from the increase to the science budget, they are essentially small-scale initiatives added on to what is already there.

No doubt they will produce some positive effects, but they are likely to have little impact on the major barriers to innovation and to creating more entrepreneurial universities in Britain.

So far, the mechanisms through which policy is delivered have not formed part of the government's agenda. However, it is in these areas where fundamental change is needed if Britain is to improve its performance. The way in which Britain's £6 billion plus a year government R&D spending gets allocated is mired in bureaucracy, and funding decisions bear no significant relation to its innovation policy agenda. The large number of government-funded schemes promoting business-academic links remains confusing to industry. The remit and future funding of the higher education sector seems to have been 'parked' in the wake of the debate on tuition fees, but lack of finance is still strangling universities' ability to upgrade.

The government says it wants more British universities and businesses to learn from the experience of universities with strong track records of commercial exploitation. This is 'motherhood and apple pie' but it is nonetheless absolutely right to do so. It is equally obvious that government cannot do everything itself and there need to be separate agendas for universities and business too. Nevertheless, government shares a responsibility for ensuring that there are 'proper systems' in place and it needs to do more to bring this about. Innovation crosses the boundaries of a number of different government departments and co-ordination of policy is an issue. There are strong vested interests within government departments and the academic community which will need to be overcome if an entrepreneurially focused innovation policy is to be rigorously implemented in Britain.

★ ★ ★ ★ ★ ★ ★ ★ ★ ★

The new government's agenda on competitiveness and innovation has rightly recognised that Britain's universities need to raise their game and be better at commercially exploiting the knowledge base.

Its policies to encourage improved performance are relatively modest however and it needs to grasp the nettle on reforming research funding, simplifying government programmes, and clarifying and differentiating roles in the higher education sector.

5. Further Areas For Action

Entrepreneurial spirit has somehow been misplaced in Britain over the last two decades or more. The motivation to create and produce new and innovative products has been lost. A gentle suffocation of innovation[1] in much of the corporate sector has been accompanied by an academic community largely disengaged from business, conducting 'blue skies' research frequently with little or no practical relevance. Government has compounded the problem through not having clear objectives or focus, and by overlaying research funding with pointless bureaucracy. The consequences of this tripartite failure for economic performance are obvious and explain why the renewal of British industries still appears fragile and spotty.[2]

Of course, this exaggerates the true picture. The science base in Britain is recognised worldwide for its quality. Britain has world-class companies, particularly in the pharmaceutical industry, which are strong in research and development and have a long track record of innovation. But it clearly is not doing nearly well enough. As knowledge becomes ever more critical to economic success, Britain has to compete through its universities as well as through its businesses. The best of them are already starting to become magnets for high technology clusters. The challenge is to broaden and deepen that success and extend it to other areas.

Change is required across the board if Britain is going to maximise the potential of its higher education sector. The United States provides a guide, but certainly not a blueprint. Britain has to find its own solution. The new government has started to tackle some of the problems. The boost to the science and engineering budget, the launch of the University Challenge fund to encourage commercial spin-offs from research and a range of other initiatives[3] demonstrate a commitment to getting it right. But more needs to be done and not just by government. The study points to seven areas where action can be taken.

1. Promote culture change and increase competition between universities.
Universities need to get with the global programme and change their culture. Stuffy, traditional and non-competitive with poor links to the business world is how the typical American undergraduate sees Britain's elite universities. Of course, this is a caricature, but it has the ring of truth to it. So too does the comment of a chairman of a major plc that universities are 'Britain's last great nationalised industry'. Some universities have moved a long way towards modernising themselves, but, for a significant number, the process is glacially slow, if apparent at all. A culture change needs to take place at all levels; from degree teaching through to research, in departments and faculties, and in every aspect of the institutions themselves.

More competition between universities for students, for the best academics, and for business is also needed. American Ivy League universities aggressively pitch against each other for the best young minds. They sell courses on their quality and on future earnings potential. They compete to hire high profile professors and top researchers, and to bring in money and projects from business. British universities do not do anything like this to the same extent. They need to. Competition between universities will only breed a better product. The guiding philosophy should be to 'denationalise' the industry, giving universities the freedom to compete, and empowering students as customers.

Transforming the culture of Britain's universities and increasing competition will not be achieved quickly and both short- and longer-term actions will be required. Initiatives that might be taken include:
- Introducing more detailed university league tables. Currently, students have very limited information at their fingertips on the quality of courses on offer. In addition to publishing information

on examination pass rates and drop out rates, each university department should be required to collect and publish details by course on the percentage of students going into jobs or research and the average starting salary. Similarly, departments should also publish key performance information relating to their research activities. League tables will give students the opportunity to make better decisions about universities and future job prospects and provide businesses with the opportunity to target the best research departments. Experience suggests they also have a galvanising effect on the institutions themselves, forcing them to reappraise, justify, improve and compete.

- Reforming the higher education funding system. The current broad funding model and bidding system should be radically overhauled to make funding follow students more closely, so that universities and departments that are successful in attracting more students get more funding than they do at the moment. In public policy, it is invariably a mistake to fund the provider rather than the purchaser, but that is essentially what the present system does. There are a number of ways it could be changed. One way would be to give students vouchers to cover the state contribution towards their education, allow universities to compete for students without pre-set limits, and allow them to charge whatever fees they felt the market would bear. A new means-tested grant regime and university bursary schemes would ensure that those from less privileged backgrounds were not prevented from taking up courses.

- Invoicing students for the cost of their education. Any change to the funding system should include making it more transparent to everyone. Students could be presented each term or each year with a bill showing the cost of their education, how much is paid by government, nationally and locally, and how much by the student or their parents. This would have a number of advantages, one of which would be to encourage students to insist on value for money not just for their contribution but for the total amount being spent. There is already some evidence that the introduction of tuition fees is making students question more what they are getting for their money, and what they can get out of it afterwards.

- Bringing in private companies to take over failing universities. The government has made clear its intentions with regard to private sector bodies being able to bid to take over failing schools. It should extend this to failing universities and further education colleges. While government does not own universities, for many, it is the dominant funder and this gives it leverage. It should be prepared to use this to drive through change.

- Stimulating the establishment of new private universities and joint ventures between universities and the private sector. Changing the rules governing the granting of university status and the power to award degrees would substantially increase private sector participation in higher education. Currently, private sector involvement is extremely limited and Britain is lagging behind not just the US but many other European countries in terms of developing academic-industry commercial partnerships. Opening up higher education to the private sector could form part of a new approach to funding and standards in the sector.

- Promoting the importance of technological education. Many of the very brightest students in the United States choose Stanford, MIT and Cal Tech over Harvard, Yale, Dartmouth and Princeton. They do so because of their reputation for excellence in mathematics, science, computing and technology – and because they want to be the next Bill Gates or Steven Jobs. In Britain, technology has traditionally tended to be seen as essentially a lower status activity. Changing this perception is not easy, but more action is clearly required if Britain is going to compete in the new technology industries. Establishing a separate, new technological university, like Stanford or MIT, is a possibility that should be considered, as should offering science and technology grants to those choosing to study in these areas.

2. Stimulate greater business involvement in academic institutions.

Business needs to recognise that universities can be a cheap source of new product ideas, innovation and recruits. There is a huge, largely latent, pool of talent at many British universities which could be accessed by business if the academic culture changed and if business realised the potential benefits of working with research teams. The corporate sector also needs to 'come out to play' and pressurise universities into becoming more business-oriented generally. Like US companies, it needs to recognise there is competitive advantage to be gained from developing closer links with the science and engineering base, forcing the pace and becoming a demanding customer. Both business and universities would benefit from:

- Better marketed, simpler programmes for industry-academic collaboration. The confusing array of current schemes need to be reviewed and rebranded and aggressively marketed. Bureaucracy needs to be kept down to a minimum. The LINK programme and the teaching company scheme have a reasonably good track record of producing tangible benefits to participating businesses and should form the backbone of a new simplified government supported system.[4] Getting more companies more involved will assist the process of building stronger partnerships, and demonstrating successful, profitable collaborations will help to expand the market. As more companies are made aware of the commercial logic in utilising academic expertise, more will want to get their slice of the action, and this will act to drive up standards.

- More business involvement on university governing councils. Many universities already have strong business input, but others do not and the overall picture is patchy. While it is not a panacea and can create problems, properly focused business involvement at the highest level can bring useful advantages, not just in terms of university management, but through concentrating attention on things that are important to them, such as decent English, competent foreign languages and high-quality business oriented courses.

- Improvement in the business content of science, engineering and IT courses. In many universities, courses need to be modified to become more business oriented. Others may need adapting as they are too oriented towards large companies and do not have a small business component, or offer modules in entrepreneurial issues. There should be more combined courses, such as management and IT.

- Transfer of good practice. Warwick Manufacturing Group is an example of what can be achieved. It is an entrepreneurial, non-for-profit organisation which is part of the University of Warwick. Turning over £80 million, less than 10 per cent comes from the Higher Education Funding Council. WMG has developed a large number of leading edge partnerships with industry in research and development, and clients include Rover/BMW, Rolls Royce and British Aerospace. It trains more than 5,000 industrialists a year and has the largest postgraduate engineering training programme in Europe. It is a model that works and there appears to be scope for replicating this approach across other industrial sectors.

- The development of a small- and medium-sized enterprise sector that is educated about changes in the knowledge economy. Innovation is making the time from drawing board to market almost disappear, and business product cycles are becoming shorter and shorter. More than ever, effective management of research and development will be critical to business success in the future. Developing strong links with university research departments should be part of the R&D strategy of any forward-looking business. Ensuring this message gets down to SMEs is important for larger companies' supply chains and for universities who need to position themselves to respond to a different set of requirements.

3. Reform government R&D funding.

Pure science is important. Any scientist can point to examples of commercial products and processes which owe their existence to serendipity and were totally unexpected spin-offs from 'basic' research. Equally, there are countless examples of British research ideas being developed and exploited elsewhere. But Britain's government has not got the R&D balance right. The nation's reputation for being good at the 'R' but bad at the 'D' is at least partly attributable to the fact that government spends very little on the latter. Less than four per cent of net government civil R&D expenditure is directed towards producing new materials, products or devices, or installing new processes, systems and services. This figure is down by a third on a decade ago, while basic research has increased.[5]

Business itself focuses its R&D resources overwhelmingly on development and on applied research. Poor linkages with government-funded research, however, are exacerbating the problem of the development gap. The government's increase in the science and engineering budget is welcome but the issue is not simply one of spending more, it is about spending it in the right areas. Profit-oriented research must stop being the exception and start being the norm. Over the short- to medium-term, government R&D funding in Britain should be reformed by:

- Shifting more funding to applied research and to tackling the development gap. This must be the priority in engineering and the physical sciences. The working assumption should be that funding would be in partnership with the private sector. Government should not be funding R&D that companies should be doing for themselves, but it needs to get closer to them than it is at the moment. For basic research, collaboration with big, world-class companies should be encouraged as it is the best way of ensuring research is at the frontier of knowledge in areas like information and communications technology.

- Concentrating funding on fewer, high quality institutions. Britain is spreading the research 'jam' too thinly and needs to concentrate resources more. In the US, research money is around eight times more concentrated than it is in Britain and this has produced far better results.[6] Moving this way will mean there will be universities which are losers, but the benefits for Britain as a whole from increasing the rate of innovation are potentially enormous if it gets it right. It will also reinforce the need for universities to be free to invent their own programmes, develop their own niches and attract their own clientele without government strings attached.

- Establishing ukinnovation.org as the first stop for all applied research and development. This body would be tasked with giving the DTI's innovation agenda the sort of 'whoosh' that has not been seen since the marketing of the Enterprise Initiative. It would take over and rationalise the current large range of separate government schemes, which are confusing to industry and academics alike, and costly to administer. The need for a separate organisation or agency to provide a clearer focus and strategy to collaborative research and development has been noted by others.[7] It is long overdue. Government should, at a minimum, bring together the current DTI and Office of Science and Technology funding streams into the new body. It should announce that its funding base will grow over time to be a higher percentage of total R&D funding than it is now, and it will need to clarify its relationship with the Research Councils to avoid any potential turf wars.

- Stripping down and refocusing research assessment. The Research Assessment Exercise (RAE) which drives the allocation of research funds has been widely criticised for failing to assess collaborative research well, particularly that undertaken with industry;[8] for being massively burdensome, and for placing too great an emphasis on publication as a measure of research quality and not enough on judging the usefulness of research.[9] Put bluntly, it is the academic paper in the learned journal that gets you the money – and professional advancement – and nothing else matters. This needs to change dramatically. For departments, collaborative research should be recognised as being, at the very least, on a par with that done by single departments, and individuals who work closely with industry valued at least as highly as those doing basic research.

4. Encourage and reward academic entrepreneurs.
To encourage profit-oriented thinking and profitable research, Britain's universities need to push researchers more into applied research, emphasising the societal as well as personal gains possible to those who create innovative products applicable to modern society. There are many ways of doing this, but the best way is always the simplest way. Government needs to make it easier and a higher priority. Universities need to regard pragmatic research as a normal part of the job description for most academic and research staff. They need also to make it easier for staff to develop businesses out of their research. Four areas in particular have been identified where action is needed:

- Change individual academic contracts to build in time which it is expected will be spent on commercial work for their private benefit. Low salaries in British universities do not help in what is increasingly becoming a war for the kind of academic talent most likely to generate spillover benefits for the economy. Studies point to a significant brain-drain to the US in 'hot' topics where academic stars are able to command huge salaries plus extensive consultancy income opportunities. The best way forward is not for government to pay more, it is to encourage academics and universities to get together with the private sector and develop a more appropriate funding mix.

- Build in incentives for university staff to act entrepreneurially to benefit the university by bringing in business sponsorship and projects. Rewarding deans, administrators, researchers, and whoever else brings in private sector money to a department, would be a positive step forward. Such schemes are fairly straightforward to introduce and police, would send out the right messages about changing the way things are done and looked at, and help address the salary gap.

- Review policies on intellectual property and patent sharing agreements to ensure they encourage spin-off businesses and offer staff and research teams incentives to exploit new ideas. There has been some improvement in the number and quality of university patent policies, but there is still catching up to be done and best practice needs to be spread.

- Encourage return tickets and easy-entries. Fluidity of movement facilitates entrepreneurship and innovation. Being able to spin out from a university and spin back if things go wrong - and often if they go right - is the hallmark of successful US technology universities and needs to happen in Britain. In the battle for talent, Britain's immigration rules are a barrier to recruiting top flight academics and technicians. They put the country at a competitive disadvantage and ways need to be found to ensure its tight rules do not put off talented academics from coming to Britain to research and to work.

5. Increase business, design and technology in schools.
Britain needs to increase the gene pool of bright young people wanting to go into high technology and engineering. But it is hampered by a schools system which is failing to give pupils sufficient experience and encouragement in this field. This has been recognised for some time, but not enough has been done. Only two out of every

hundred 12-18 year olds participate in the three principal industry link schemes. Various initiatives are underway, but they are all essentially very small-scale.[10]

It is high time government and industry in Britain combined together and really started to properly fund initiatives to make engineering and business part of the school curriculum and to promote these as careers. Despite previous initiatives, the number and proportion of students deciding to take engineering as a degree is still declining. This has serious long-term consequences. From apprentices to graduate engineers, employers cannot recruit enough of the right people to meet their future needs and this is harming competitiveness.

Government plans extending work-related learning to 14-16 year olds are to be welcomed, but they run the risk of perpetuating the image of industry being only for the low-achieving or disaffected. Britain must go much further. Science, engineering and technology need to be promoted across the ability range. The New Deal for Schools needs to address the problem that few schools have the resources or expertise to teach engineering.

6. Improve government focus and co-ordination.

The new government in Britain has made a concerted attempt to set a clear policy framework in which innovation and enterprise play a key part. Rightly, it has rejected the arguments of those who say it should just get out the way. Every other major government has policies to encourage and support innovation and Britain needs to do so as well. By its very nature, however, government is complex and different government departments have different objectives and priorities.

Innovation policy needs to cut across a range of areas. Science policy is the responsibility of DTI and the Office for Science and Technology; university financing and research funding comes mainly through Department for Education and Employment, and the research and funding councils which report to OST; European funding comes with other strings and reporting responsibilities; planning is controlled by Department for Environment, Transport and the Regions, which controls the Regional Development Agencies; the tax regime and financial incentive schemes, like Venture Capital Trusts, is the province of the Treasury, which also houses the Enterprise and Growth Unit. While not underestimating the degree of co-ordination between departments that is taking place currently, Britain would benefit from giving a higher priority to maximising the potential of the higher education sector to contribute to growth and prosperity. Establishing an inter-departmental Task Force and having a more powerful Cabinet sub-committee would be one way of facilitating stronger cross-departmental co-ordination which is obviously needed to ensure coherence.

7. Support the growth of clusters.

Universities have a key role to play in the formation and development of industry clusters. Stanford has been pivotal to the growth of Silicon Valley as a hotbed of technology companies, likewise MIT and the businesses along Route 128. The best universities can act as magnets, spawning and attracting businesses. Clustering is important because the competition, collaboration, knowledge and skills development which takes place as critical mass builds, creates competitive advantage and leads to economic growth. It is not impossible to stimulate the creation of clusters through government policy, but it is better if government action focuses on supporting established or emerging clusters.

Britain's only world-class cluster is arguably its London-based financial services industry. But there are signs of other clusters developing. High-tech industries already account for around one in five jobs in Cambridge and the surrounding area,[11] many of which are new biotechnology-based companies, and the potential for further growth linked to the university is enormous.

Britain could strengthen universities and support the growth of industry clusters through:

- Ensuring universities clearly address their role in contributing to economic growth. Britain's top universities have the capability to play a leading role in cluster development. They need to recognise their strength and play to it. Other universities need to recognise that they have a more minor but still important supporting role, principally ensuring the availability of trained technicians, managers and professionals. University 'missions' need to reflect this.

- Encouraging more venture capital funds which are targeted at funding the commercialisation of university research, and enticing more 'business angels' to invest in high-tech start-ups. The priority for government should be not to set up more new funds itself, but to encourage the private sector to do better. Britain's venture capital industry leads Europe but lags substantially behind that of the US. Moreover, two thirds of venture capital funds go into management buy-outs and other deals which are not start-up or early-stage finance. The situation is improving but too many British venture capitalists are unimaginative. Compared with their US counterparts they are on a different planet when considering what a start-up could achieve.

- Developing the infrastructure and networks to facilitate university spin-off companies. Infrastructure is as important as availability of capital in developing new innovative businesses. One of the key strengths of Silicon Valley is its infrastructure. A network of lawyers, venture capitalists, investment banks, headhunters and others make it exceptionally easy to start a new business quickly. Some of this can be attributed to advantages of scale and is not easily replicable, but there are signs it is beginning to happen around Cambridge.[12] In other parts of Britain, however, different models will be required. The government's new Small Business Service should have as one of its objectives encouraging start-ups from university research. Britain's universities also need to review the organisations they have set up to commercialise research. Too many lack the size to do a good job. They should look to collaborate together, possibly on a regional basis, creating a single body with the range of skills and contacts required to go out and find academics and research teams with patentable ideas and help turn them into a commercial reality.

- Changing planning law to allow cluster development. Britain's planning regulations are an obstacle to expansion. They need to be reformed so that nascent clusters are not strangled by over-restrictive policies to protect the green belt.

- Expanding and creating more science and research parks. The demand needs first to be there to do this, but, where it is, such parks can support the development of new technology-based businesses. Proximity to the university is important and can help the development of collective learning networks as businesses grow. A rigorous approach needs to be taken to ensure these parks only let premises to university spin-offs, or other companies with real academic links.

* * * * * * * * * *

Britain has a big advantage over most other countries in the quality of its science base and its elite universities. The challenge it faces is to maximise the potential of the higher education sector to contribute to growth and prosperity. To compete successfully in the fast moving, global, knowledge driven markets of the next millennium, Britain needs innovative and entrepreneurial universities conducting world-class research, and strong incentives and mechanisms to ensure that research is systematically exploited commercially.

Meeting this challenge will require some fundamental changes. The new Labour government has made a start, but it should be much more radical. The study points to seven areas where action is needed and highlights a range of initiatives which could be taken. Some of these are highly controversial and strong vested interests will need to be overcome if substantial progress is to be made. Action will, however, produce long-term benefits for Britain's economy.

The danger for Britain is to think that such radical action is not needed. Improvements are being made. There is progress which can be pointed to. But Britain's universities are way off the pace when it comes to developing links with businesses, acting innovatively and commercialising research. And, what is more, they are falling further and further behind. The nation that cultivated the first industrial revolution is in danger of losing out on the new, global technological revolution that is driving the start of the new millennium. The raw materials are there, but change is needed if Britain is to create a strong innovative economy. Many already recognise this, but they cannot do it alone. The task now is for government to act in partnership with the private sector and with universities to make it happen.

Notes

Chapter 1

1. As the analysis and background paper to the Competitiveness White Paper, DTI (1998), rightly points out, Alfred Marshall wrote over a century ago that 'knowledge is our most powerful engine of production'. Despite this, classical growth theory assumed knowledge and technological progress was an exogenous variable. While this was challenged by those such as Schumpeter (1934,1942), it was basically accepted as conventional wisdom. From a variety of perspectives, however, the importance of technology and human capital as a determinant of growth is now widely recognised. See for example Solow (1957), Krugman (1980), Helpman and Krugman (1985) and Porter (1990). Crafts (1996) from a technical perspective looks at the policy implications of new growth theory. A recent study, Aghion and Howitt (1998), provides a detailed analysis and explanation of endogenous growth and looks set to be a standard text. For a critique of endogenous growth theory's importance, see Jones (1995).
2. Britain's ranking is well-known in terms of output per capita. In any economy, output per capita is determined by total factor productivity in the long run. The McKinsey Global Institute study (1998) highlights low labour productivity as where Britain particularly falls behind its competitors.
3. See McKinsey, op cit.
4. In certain sectors and markets, economies of scale or scale efficiencies contribute to making some firms or industries more competitive than others. The size of the US market has long

been held to be an advantage for its companies. Given more global competition and freer markets, however, this factor is declining in its overall importance.
5. McKinsey argue that 'low skills have often been overcome by best-practice operators using tailored processes and intensive job-specific training programmes'. They use this reason to justify low skills levels being an 'important secondary effect' rather than a primary root cause of economic problems (p.vi). While some world-class, British-based companies may be able to do this, there is substantial evidence that skills are highly important and that Britain does have a 'skills gap' with its major competitors.
6. See HM Treasury (1998) Pre-Budget Report for an exposition.
7. As noted above, the Government's recognition of modern growth theory runs through all its major policy statements. Labour's commitment to this pre-dates government, as Gordon Brown's much publicised speech mentioning 'post-neoclassical endogenous growth theory' demonstrates.
8. The quote is from Porter (1990) whose analysis of the determinants of national competitive advantage is very much of relevance to government.
9. Peter Hall's (1998) incredibly broad and sophisticated book *Cities in Civilisation* makes this point (p. 498).
10. The possible exceptions are Renaissance Florence and Tokyo. Hall, *op cit*, however, notes the importance of skills and education in Florence which made it 'both highly literate, and yet preserved from a scholastic straightjacket' (p. 89). He also points out that while innovation in Japan has been driven by large corporations, governmental vision and guidance have been crucial, and universities have produced the top-level labour force required for innovation to take place (pp. 455-482). Both these 'exceptions' reinforce the relevance of this study's focus.

Chapter 2

1. Britain's perceived failure to turn inventions into innovations has long attracted concern. The ESRC is currently funding a three-year research project at the University of Edinburgh to investigate the problem. James Dyson's cyclone bagless cleaning system is a recent example of a British invention having to go abroad to find commercial backing. British scientific advances in medical instrument technology, such as the body scanner, have also been exploited outside the country. Separate but related to this are examples where British inventions were originally exploited by British companies, but where the country no longer has a market presence. Television is an example. Although there are companies making televisions in Britain, none are British owned.
2. Patent performance and R&D expenditure are widely held to be highly significant determinants of innovative capacity. Other measures, such as the number of scientific publications, are interesting but clearly less important.
3. This is a key finding of Michael Porter's recent work with Scott Stern on developing an Innovation Index. See Porter (1998).
4. Porter (1998). Figures again are on a per capita basis.
5. This is evident from OECD statistics. Charts 2.3 and 2.4 which follow and are drawn from Science, Education and Technology Statistics (1999) illustrate the argument.
6. The R&D Scoreboard covers around 500 UK companies who report R&D expenditure in their annual accounts. A similar procedure is used for other countries to allow international comparisons to be made. The top 20 UK companies account for two-thirds of the total spend recorded by the R&D Scoreboard.
7. The breakdowns of R&D expenditure used are according to the OECD Frascati manual. Strategic applied research is defined as applied research where the work, although directed toward practical aims, has not yet advanced to the stage where eventual

applications can be clearly specified. The manual also provides more detailed descriptions of the terms basic research, specific applied research, and experimental referred to above, as well as other categories. See SET (1999) pp. 2-3.
8. See SET (1999) Table 3.4.

Chapter 3

1. Lord Robbins was chairman of the Committee on Higher Education established by the Prime Minister in 1961 and reporting in 1963. Its review led to the first wave of expansion of higher education.
2. The statistics are taken from the Dearing Report (1997) pp. 18-23.
3. Dearing, *op cit*, p. 17.
4. Clutterbuck and Crainer (1988) p. 76 make this specific point. See also Barnett (1987) and Elbaum and Lazonick (1986) for critiques. Porter (1990) also notes how Britain's education system has lagged badly behind other advanced nations.
5. Elbaum and Lazonick (1986).
6. Michael Porter (1990) makes this point forcibly in his analysis of 'the slide of Britain.' See p. 498.
7. The growth of involvement of the private sector in US universities was largely the result of Federal withdrawal of funding for civil research and development. It forced universities to search around for other sources of funding.
8. Around 30,000 students participate in Young Enterprise, 16,000 in Young Engineers and 15,500 in CREST according to DTI.
9. See James Aley (1997) for a flavour of just how different attitudes are in the US compared with Britain.
10. The image and status of engineering in Britain has consistently been a cause for concern. Government, the CBI, the EEF and others have all introduced action plans and other initiatives with very limited impact. Pay is an issue in attracting top graduates.

City starting salaries for graduates are around £25,000 compared with about £18,000 for top business recruits, with the salary gap widening over time.
11. This observation comes from Burton Clark (1988) and his interesting analysis of pathways to organisational transformation in European universities.
12. Memorandum submitted to House of Commons Science and Technology Committee. See Minutes of Evidence, Monday 1 February 1999.
13. The quotation is from Goodwin and Matthews (1988).
14. See TCS Quinquennial Review (1997). The SMART and SPUR awards schemes have also been favourably evaluated.
15. This was the common response from those submitting evidence to Dearing (1997) and is reflected in their final report.
16. Cambridge, one of the most advanced and organised, for instance has the Wolfson Industrial Liaison Office and a company Cambridge University Technical Services Ltd. There is also Cambridge Research and Innovation Ltd. Manchester University has VUMAN Ltd which is similar to CUTS. Bristol University has Bristol Innovations Ltd. Nothing in Britain, however, remotely approaches the scale of Stanford.
17. Figures quoted by the Association of University Teachers.
18. See Professor Sir Alec Broers' evidence to Science and Technology Committee, 1 February 1999, pp. 232-233.
19. See Aley (1997) and Pfeiffer (1997) for commentaries on competition between US universities and between companies for university talent.
20. Reported in Times Higher Education Supplement, 10 July 1998 and 14 August 1998.

Chapter 4

1. For more detailed information on the new measures introduced in Britain since 1997 see the 1999 Budget red book. HM Treasury also has a useful website.
2. The Minister responsible for biotechnology is Lord Sainsbury.
3. The new schemes announced are summarised in the 1998 competitiveness white paper. See DTI (1998).
4. The observation that Britain needs an innovation policy which takes a broader view than science and technology policy is not new. See Porter (1990) p. 691.

Chapter 5

1. Kanter (1984) wrote about the 'quiet suffocation' of the entrepeneurial spirit in American segmentalist companies. It is equally true of much of the British corporate sector today, though there are obviously honourable exceptions. Her analysis of innovation and the role of corporate entrepreneurs remains extremely powerful.
2. Porter (1990) observed this of British industry at the end of the 1980s. One decade on and little appears to have changed.
3. See the 17 March 1998 budget press release statement on the £50m University Challenge fund (DTI, P/98/222) and the Comprehensive Spending Review announcement on the £1.1 billion boost for science (DTI, P/98/567).
4. See for instance PACEC (1996) and the TCS Quinquennial review (1997).
5. Science, Engineering & Technology Statistics (1997), Table 3.5.
6. Shattock (1998) notes that 35 per cent of university science and technology research funding is concentrated in 0.7 per cent of institutions and 96 per cent of all research monies in 5.5 per cent, with the comparable figures for Britain being 4.4 per cent and 39 per cent. He notes the figures are distorted by medical research,

but perceptively questions whether research is sufficiently concentrated to hold off European competition.
7. The Dearing Report called for an Industrial Partnership Development Fund. Goodwin and Matthews (1998) from Warwick Manufacturing Group have argued for a National Innovation Agency. The suggestions are similar, though the latter propose incorporating Research Council funding into the single stream, not just DTI/OST funding. This would clearly be highly controversial and is probably something best considered as a possible second stage.
8. Dearing (1997), para 11.71.
9. For example, see House of Commons Science & Technology Committee (1998) p. XXIX.
10. The 1994 Action for Engineering initiative and the Yes to Engineering Success scheme sought to address the need to build links between industry and schools and promoting the attractiveness of engineering as a career. Both however were very small scale. Quinco, a charitable company aiming to encourage engineering recruits, took over from YES in 1998 and will receive up to £200,000 for each of the next three years from the DTI to support its work. See the press information: Action Plans from Action for Engineering (DTI, P/95/802); Ian Taylor gives the green light to the Year of Engineering Success (DTI, P/96/667); and, for Quinco, Revolution sets new challenges for Engineers (DTI, P/98/573).
11. Estimates suggest high-tech industries account for 15 per cent of jobs in Cambridge and 24 per cent in South Cambridgeshire, the district surrounding the town, Financial Times, 3 August 1998.
12. Cambridge has attracted a number of venture capital funds and a growing number of accountancy and law firms have established offices there. For recent comment see Financial Times, 29/30 August 1998.

Bibliography

Aghion, Philippe and Howitt, Peter, *Endogenous Growth Theory*, The MIT Press, Cambridge, Massachusetts, 1998.
Aley, James, 'The Heart of Silicon Valley', *Fortune*, July 7, 1997.
Bank of England, *Finance for Small Firms*, A fourth report, January 1997.
Bank of England, *The Financing of Technology-based Small Firms*, October 1996.
Barnett, Correlli, *The Pride and the Fall : The Dream and Illusion of Britain as a Great Nation*, New York: The Free Press, 1987.
Clark, Burton R., *Creating Entrepreneurial Universities*, Pergamon, 1998.
Clutterbuck, D. and Crainer, S., *The Decline and Rise of British Industry*, London: WH Allen & Co., 1988.
Confederation of British Industry, *Tech Stars*, February 1997.
Coopers & Lybrand International, *Globalisation in the new millennium: success strategies for high tech companies*, UK:Sceptre Litho, June 1996.
Crafts, Nick, 'Post-Neoclassical Endogenous Growth Theory: What are its Policy Implications?', *Oxford Review of Economic Policy*, Vol.12, No.2, 1996.
CVCP, *Research in Universities: The Funding Gap*, 1997.
Dearing Report, *Higher Education in the Learning Society*, The National Committee of Inquiry into Higher Education, July 1997.
Department for Education and Employment, *Higher Education for the 21st Century: Response to the Dearing Report*, HMSO, February 1998.
Department of Trade and Industry, *Building the Knowledge Driven Economy*, Competitiveness White Paper, Cm4176, December 1998.
Department of Trade and Industry, *Foresight*, HMSO: March 1998.

Department of Trade and Industry, *Foresight in business: Winning Advantage*, HMSO: February 1998.
Department of Trade and Industry, *Foresight in business: Winning Advantage*, HMSO: March 1997.
Department of Trade and Industry, *Realising our potential: A strategy for Science, Engineering and Technology*, HMSO: May 1993.
Elbaum and Lazonick, *The Decline of the British Economy*, Oxford: 1986.
Goodwin, Tom and Mathews, Nick, *Knowledge Transfer: A UK Competitive Weakness*, U.K.: Institute of Public Policy Research, 1998.
Hall, Peter, *Cities in Civilization*, Weidenfield & Nicolson, London, 1998.
Hamilton, Joan O' C., and Himelstein, L., 'A Wellspring Called Stanford' *Business Week*, August 25 1997.
Harvey, Kerron (ed), *Research Partnerships between industry and Universities: a guide to better practice*, UK: AURIL/CBI, 1997.
Helpman, E. and Krugman, Paul R, *Market Structure and Foreign Trade: Increasing Returns, Imperfect Competition and the International Economy*, Cambridge. MIT Press, 1985.
HM Treasury, *The Pre-Budget Report*, 1998.
HM Treasury, *Innovating for the Future: Investing in R&D*, consultation document, 17 March 1998.
HM Treasury, *The Financing of High Technology Companies*, 1998.
House of Commons Science and Technology Committee, *The Implications of the Dearing Report for the Structure and Funding of University Research*, HMSO: 25 March 1998.
Jones, C. I., 'R&D Based Models of Economic Growth', *Journal of Political Economy*, 103: 759-84, 1995.
Kanter, Rosabeth Moss, *The Change Masters: corporate entrepreneurs at work*, London: George Allen & Unwin, 1984.
Keeble, D., Lawson, C., Lawton Smith, H., Moore, B. and Wilkinson, F., *Collective Learning Processes and Inter-firm Networking in*

Innovative High-Technology Regions, ESRC Centre for Business Research, Cambridge, 1998.

Krugman, Paul R., 'Scale Economies, Product Differentiation, and the Pattern of Trade', *American Economic Review*, Vol. 70, No. 5, 1980.

McKinsey Global Institute, *Driving Productivity Growth in the UK Economy*, 1998.

McKenna, Regis, 'Rating the Regions: Our experts call it!!: Leading the nation by a wide margin is Silicon Valley', *Forbes*, August 25 1997.

Moore, I. and Garnsey,E., 'Funding for innovation in small firms: the role of Government', *Research Policy 22*, 1993.

National Audit Office, *The Department of Trade and Industry's Support for Innovation*, 1995.

PACEC, *The Economic Impact and Operational Effectiveness of the Teaching Company Scheme*, Public & Corporate Economic Consultants, Cambridge, 1996.

Pfeiffer, Eric, 'What MIT Learned from Stanford', *Forbes*, August 25 1997.

Porter, Michael E., 'Competitiveness in the UK: The Innovation Challenge', Lecture, QEII Conference Centre, London, 10 December 1998.

Porter, Michael E., 'Clusters and the New Economics of Competition', *Harvard Business Review*, November-December 1998.

Porter, Michael E., *The Competitive Advantages of Nations*, London: Macmillian,1990.

Sanderson, M., *The Universities and British Industry, 1850-1970*, London: Routledge & Kegan Paul, 1972.

Schumpeter, Joseph A., *The Theory of Economic Development*, Cambridge, Harvard University Press, 1934.

Schumpeter, Joseph A., *Capitalism, Socialism and Democracy*, New York: Harper and Row, 1942.

Science, Engineering and Technology Statistics 1997, UK, HMSO, July 1998.

Shattock, Michael, 'The Challenge Ahead', *Times Higher Education Supplement*, 14 August 1998.

Solow, Robert, 'Technological Change and the Aggregate Production Function', *The Review of Economics and Statistics*, Vol. 39, No. 3, 1957.

TCS Quinquennial Review, *1996 TCS Quinquennial Review*, Report of the Review Panel and Government's response, July 1997.

The Times, *Good University Guide*, Times Books, London, 1997.

United States Department Of Education, *Current Year Finance Report*, final release, 1995.

University of Oxford, *Research at Oxford: The Sciences*, Oxford, 1998.

Weiner, Martin J., *English Culture and the Decline of the Industrial Spirit 1850-1980*, Cambridge University Press, 1981.

Wilkinson, R., *The Prefects: British Leadership and the Public School Tradition*, London: Oxford University Press, 1985.

Williamson, Oliver E., *Markets and Hierarchies: Analysis and Anti-trust Implications*.